FIREFLIES

MERCER
UNIVERSITY PRESS

Endowed by

TOM WATSON BROWN

and

THE WATSON-BROWN FOUNDATION, INC.

Fireflies

POEMS

John Leland

Mercer University Press | MACON, GEORGIA

MUP/P521

Published by Mercer University Press
1501 Mercer University Drive
Macon, Georgia 31207

9 8 7 6 5 4 3 2 1

Books published by Mercer University Press are printed on acid-free paper that meets the requirements of the American National Standard for Information Sciences—Permanence of Paper for Printed Library Materials.

ISBN 978-0-88146-550-1
Cataloging-in-Publication Data is available from the Library of Congress

For Celia

Contents

Like a cat

Like a cat,
I lay this mangled corpse at your feet:
My daughter dancing through the forest of years,
forever a child in the dream of the huntsman
who must kill the wolves in the woods
and marry the witch who keeps her caged in her hate.
For you I have killed her;
here she is at your feet,
wrapped in a dream.
Remember me when you eat her.

On Song

Biology calls them the living dead—
so isolated reproductively
they'll have no offspring to remember them.
Like you, old bullfrog, whose voyage overland

to this Easter Island of a swamp
would be *Ranid* legend, were other than
promiscuous cicadas and tree frogs
audience. Grown old jug-jugarumping

to a bog indifferent to your song,
you chant half-heartedly your requiem
out more of habit than of hope, and quit,
resigned tonight to personal extinction.

Memories

The magic box we rode still rises
to the floor where stuffed animals
stare from their glass enclosures,
turtle and porpoise swim the air,

the platypus's stuffing leaks,
lion and lamb lie down together,
and the dinosaurs' plaster tracks
stalk the empty basement halls.

Desert roses bloom in stone,
and the slowly turning seismograph,
unperturbed though you have grown,
records earthquakes in Japan.

Ghost nets

Awful shadows float unseen the oceans
of our world, miles long and fathoms deep,
ensnaring crabs, fish, seals, porpoise and penguin,
leviathan himself—fish, flesh, and fowl,
whatever swims the sea. Cast or cut off
by accident or storm, and gorged with catch,
such nets descend to depths and darknesses
where misshapen denizens devour the dead.
Lightened, they rise, fill and sink and rise again,
and fill and sink and rise, and fill and sink
as long as their unrotting meshes hold.
Befouled with barnacles and seaweeds
and sun-bleached carapace and bone,
their tangled wreckage strewn upon the beach
is lethal cousin to the twenty feet
of ragged cotton hung with oars and starfish
that catch our dining eyes in restaurants,
and less terrible than the seine of sorrow
that hauled my father, dead these twenty years,
unbidden from within me when I cursed
my son in my father's voice and words,
dragging him to the abyss where my voice,
disembodied like my father's, now floats,
a nightmare trawling my son's memory.

Legacy

Laid in a land our people have manured
for centuries, my father's body sinks
through this spit of sand where nothing grows
but pine, the water vanishing like dust
between the grains—leaf, limb and his decay
leaching to the seeps below to nourish
vegetable monstrosities so deprived
so long they dreamed themselves carnivorous:
Dionaea's trip-wired traps, meat-colored,
snake quick; *Sarracena*'s deceiving udders
swollen, sweet-scented, drugged and dangerous;
Drosera's tentacled rosettes glinting
like shattered glass, their viscid dew drops dining
on those that think to drink—what once was leaf
twisted by a need so naked into something
we dared not dream, not even in nightmare.

Casting

My father could so throw
a cotton cast net
that it caught the sun itself
in flight and hung suspended
in the summer sky,
till time fell heavy
as a winter shawl
upon an old man's shoulders
and he could catch no more
the children of the creek.

Mired in the mud of middle age
I but mimic him,
his stance, his age, his cast,
trawling memory's hole
for whatever lurks below,
and, as my tide ebbs, read
in the vague tug of twined thread
the terrors of the trapped,
then draw them, slowly,
towards sunlight and death.

Cocktails

I now know what you knew then
when you sat evenings sipping Scotch
as bitter as the cud you chewed,
that this is all there is, this,
this body, family, these walls,
how disappointed one is
when middle age's lowering clouds
close in on one's horizons,
how preferable to strike at those
around one rather than oneself.

Bedtime

My son climbs
with his teddy
into bed:

"I am scared,
Daddy, scared."
So we nestle,

he laying
his child's body
next to mine,

my ex-wife's
admonition,
"He's too old

still to be
sleeping with you,"
here too.

And she's right,
yet here he is,
tonight, with me,

gracing bed
with what remains
of faith in father.

Your first bike ride

Watching you ride off down the street
without a backward glance my way,
I fret as any parent might

about what you will face when gone
beyond my care, what careless cars
and snarling dogs may threaten then,

what fears you'll dread despite my love,
and selfishly suppose it like
the day you leave me in the grave.

Root crops

Come spring, we plant.
I dig the holes
and Edward drops in
eyed potatoes
we bury in the dirt.
Come fall, we hunt,
me with the spade
and Edward sifting
for buried treasure,
insisting now,
we eat them now,
Daddy, right now,
And so we do,
baked, fried, or boiled,
whatever he wants,
burying within him
memories to feast
upon in future years.

Continental drift

Once I sat and took my child,
her hand in mine, and cut her nails,
the slivers of her childhood fell
like crescents of a waning moon.

She and I grow distant now,
as slowly as her nails grow out,
slow as divorcing continents,
as moons escape a world's embrace.

The earth itself once rose in tides
when its moon loomed larger overhead.
Such times are gone, and though the land
forget, the seas remember yet,

and continents' outlines recall
their former unions, and my soul
rises like the tide when I behold
my child, grown distant though we be.

Report card

My son's kindergarten teacher wrote
in cursive typical of such as she:
"Edward shows significant improvement
in having learned to keep within the lines he
colors." Don't we all, eventually,
so circumscribe ourselves with others' lines:
yes ma'am, no sir, please, mother may I,
Simon says, and no you can't, and mind
you do just as I say, this where the plate
and knife and you must go, this the way
to pray to god, and this the god you pray
to, this the soap you use, and this the state
you pledge allegiance to, this the abuse
you take, and these the rules of poetry you use.

Absence

Startled, sometimes she came upon it mornings,
his failed and fading ghost
pale as a face within a window pane,
what should have been a something to a someone
an absence haunting a hole
dug by what it wasn't—a presence.

Weekend visitation

Emptied of whatever once was valued,
bottles flung from our world's bridges shatter
in shards sharp enough to slice my daughter's
bare beachcombing feet, save that they've suffered
a sea change into something rich and strange:
pennies beer bottle-brown and clouded green,
cobalt blue, yellow, red, and turquoise coins,
sea glass ubiquitous as pocket change.
Like archeologists we puzzle out
what vanished shapes they took, what spaces filled,
what miracles their fragile walls contained,
their ragged edges so sea-sanded smooth
that even God might not join together
what careless men and women broke asunder.

Brothers

Back when I shared a bedroom with my brother,
sleep was perilous. Outside the windows
branches snaked, beneath our bunk bed, monsters
lurked, and God forbid we fail to close
tight the closet door, sealing off
whatever lived within. Such things scent us,
tracking back to open mouths trails of
human-flavored CO2, our slumbers
safe only under cover, where we choke
on our effluvia. Wrapped in my fear
and blankets, cocooned in air that stank
of me, I never told my sleeping brother,
who little dreamed his head, naked to the night
celestial, was his brother's monster bait.

Home thoughts

Sometimes the net will snag an orphan pot,
its buoy cut loose by a careless boater,
and then you have to wade in, the water
grey, cool, and dark, rising to your armpits,
reach down, and gingerly haul out your net
and wayward pot, within which lurks a crab
grown enormous eating captive crabs,
the cannibal survivor of a feast
of generations, each seduced in turn
by those that, starving, tear their fellows' sides,
the scent of carcass spreading on the tide,
attracting eager predators that crawl
and clamber to their muddy deaths until
but one lonely lunatic remains.

Toadfish

Stuck in a tank in Iowa
a thousand miles from mud and creek,
an oyster toadfish sings at night,
his lab illuminated by
an exit sign rising red
as the moon over closed doors.
Tomorrow gloved hands will grasp
him very carefully behind
his poisoned fins and pointed teeth,
and sacrifice him for research.
But tonight, he sings, a foghorn
shipwrecked on the prairie,
remembering, remembering.

Old Glory

1

You don't need much to make a flag, a sheet
of paper, white, two crayons, red and blue,
and a pattern. Across America,
children possessed by such a pattern draw,
as perfectly as second graders can,
red rectangles they fit with thirteen stripes,
though most fudge the number, and a blue box,
upper left, to house the fifty stars,
hard even if you leave mere dots for stars,
impossible if you have learned the art
of drawing them with one unbroken line.

2

Flying the flag's one thing they can't forbid,
so auto dealers fly garrison flags,
nylon sheets twenty feet by thirty eight,
cheaper than billboards at a thousand bucks,
big enough to build on, and arresting,
which is the point, when lifted by the wind,
but so extravagant I find myself
calculating how many kites and panties
you could cut from so much polyester.

3

You're supposed to raise and lower, fold
such flags in ceremonies fixed by rules
whose steps I learned and then forgot while yet

a Boy Scout, remembering only this,
that you must so fold the flag upon itself
you're left with a triangle fret with stars,
like that the military gave us
when my father died, a cotton flag
five feet by nine that lay ignored years
within my bureau drawer where it looked
like nothing other than a rumpled shirt,
until I gave my son my father's flag
which he unfurled and flies upon his wall.

4

Jim Berger grew his prison flag from scraps
of scavenged cloth. He'd time enough, six years,
to puzzle how to cut so what he cut
was flag, and not a tattered rag, carving
into cloth a silhouette of absence,
invisible when, as told, he folded
so his captors saw, as saw they must,
a handkerchief. But Berger rose before
his captors rose, took from his clothes the cloth
and with a red scrap colored in the stripes
and blued the canton with a sock. Standing
as he had learned in elementary school,
Berger squared his shoulders, pledged the pledge,
and flew his flag, forbidden, in Hanoi.

Teachers

Every May, Virginia mourns her dead.
And every May we teachers watch
others' ever younger children
repeat the old, old story
they have learned
so well, so very, very well:
died on the field of honor, sir,
died on the field of honor.

Year after year,
their names, ordinary as any
classroom roll—Atwill, Cabel, Crockett,
Hartsfield, Haynes, Jefferson,
Jones, McDowell, Stanard, Wheelwright—
stick in our silent throats
while we watch others' children die.

Year after year
they pass us by,
we who remain,
we who remain silent,
repeating the old, old story,
died on the field of honor, sir,
died on the field of honor.

Collateral damage

How many box turtles die summer nights
beneath the wheels of teenage boys intent
on perfecting the art of ricochet,
hitting with their cars' front tires the shells just right,
so the turtles spin safely through the air
like their cartoon kin, mere millimeters
the difference between success and failure.
It's difficult at sixty miles an hour
to precisely aim, when drunk, a two-ton
moving vehicle, what with the roadbed,
crawling turtle, a girlfriend's halfhearted
please don'ts distracting from the task at hand.
Stuff happens, as Sunday morning's roadkill
testifies. But tonight, let's roll, let's roll.

Lessons

Beneath the half-mast flag commemorating
yet another graduate dead in war
cadets in camo crawl the grass, cradling
rifles, watched over by instructors
fresh from the front themselves. Was he one,
when radar-dodging fighter jets flew low,
who rushed the windows in delight, one
who found the rifle range's staccato
more poetic than pentameters,
who spied his face among those charging skyward
in the chapel, who dreamed his name in bronze?
The name's familiar, but the face I find
in an old yearbook not one I know,
nor one that learned what then I thought I knew.

Pheremones

They caught your eye, their green and yellow shapes,
and brought you in. So seductive were their
guarantees that you bought six, hung and watched
swarms of hard-shelled and horny beetles
seduced and clambering on the lures fall
into the waiting bags. So many bags
you emptied, turning the stinking carcasses
into the soil where their metallic green
and gold still lie in undecaying piles.
Lured too, though this the store failed to mention,
a thousand pregnant females, all who laid
their eggs within your garden's walls, the ground
alive this summer with corpse-colored grubs
inviting in turn moles whose tunnels undermine
your rows and invite hungry voles to feast
upon your fruit and vegetables. The cure?
An electronic vole and mole control,
batteries included, guaranteed to work.

The Shenandoah Sea

When temperature inversions fill with fog
the Valley, islanding Short Hills, North, Jump,
and House mountains, I can almost see
Thomas Jefferson's imagined ocean

filling the Shenandoah to its brim,
a thirty-mile-wide, thousand-foot-deep gulf
whose cataclysmic overspilling cut
the Shenandoah and Potomac rivers

and made Harper's Ferry "sublime enough
to cross an ocean for," topography
the record of the war of rock and water,
and spectral falls, but barely dry, metaphor

for revolution. And one which science
soon evaporated, even Jefferson
repudiating cataclysm
for uniformitarianism,

the belief that what we see is caused but
by the forces that we know, the fossil
trilobites and corals, brachiopods
and star-shaped crinoids he saw littering

the Valley's limestones left so long ago
the ocean they had populated dried
and blew away before the rivers carved
the valley he imagined once a sea.

Yet when trucks hum like surf on 81,
and ailanthus hang palmlike in the haze,
I too taste salt and dream myself beachcombing
for sea shells among the Valley's beeches.

Decay

You come upon such ruins in the woods,
their wooden flooring, walls, and roofs long gone
to fire and decay, the chimney's stones
collapsed into the soil from which they rose,

this sunken ground the root cellar, now filled
with leaves and loam, these the foundation stones
and these the unswept stoop and backdoor stones,
and through this nothingness which once was wall

you spy the maples having breeched the pasture
fence and occupied the field. The chimney's
sandstone browns and reds have dulled as grey
as dying dreams, now the only color

the daffodils lifting their drowning heads
above the leaves, the yucca's ghostly
candles lighting moths their solitary
ways, and the periwinkle's purple shroud.

The Abortion

Having ogled in museums
as in a carnie sideshow things
like you drowned in formaldehyde,
I blush when through the wall I hear
the toilet rush as years ago
it rushed when you, my child, were flushed,
dead and disjointed like a chicken,
into the sewers of my soul.

The Pond

The pond floated first within your mind
as perfect as a kitchen calendar's.
It took the backhoe days to grub a bowl,
to scrape away the valley's skin of clay
draped over hidden limestone ledges,
and dam the creek. Downstream, the creek bed dried,
unmade and rumpled, filled with detritus,
groundhogs burrowing where once water ran.
Clear and clean and deep enough to skinny dip,
the blue-eyed water you'd impounded clouded
with sediment as slowly as a cataract,
its bottom thickening with last year's leaves,
green and purple algae coughed up like phlegm.
Each pint's pound of water depressed the ground
it lay upon, sieving through the limestone,
until your dream died drip by unseen drip,
evaporating like a sun-struck puddle,
its bass and bluegill stinking in the light,
only this snapping turtle, wrinkle-necked
and draped with duckweed, muck incarnate,
crawling towards other, darker depths
dimly imagined in its reptile mind.

A Dying Tree

Older trees, like this *Pawlonia*,
were once living posts for fencers
too rushed to plant a proper fence,
their bark scarred and gnarled by wire
and nail, and some few like this one
rung with wire where the farmer
looped and cinched a turn to tighten
a sagging fence or take a corner,
the tree's thickening trunk disguising
with double chins the choking necklace,
each year's growth tightening the garrot,
each spring another leafless branch
grasping arthritically the air,
each summer fewer panicles
to mourn the passing of a tree.

Cutting the Calves

He came in spring to cut the calves,
herding them into the pen,
their lowing mothers left outside,
and steered the bull calves, one by one,

into the chute and scissored gate
that held them tightly in a head lock.
Then reaching through the slats, he squeezed
the testicles against the sac,

and sawing sideways through the bag,
pulled out their balls, freed and tossed
them to the dogs, who ate their fill
and left the rest for fly and buzzard.

Rumpelstiltskin

That summer we backed wagon on wagon
into the loft, our contesting boys
heaving ever higher bale upon square bale,
till in the central bay a hay cathedral
rose through the sunbeam-shafted gloom
to where the praising pigeons clapped their wings.

Below the wild cat's litter tussled
in a tangle of cobweb and broken twine,
swallows bubble-gummed their nests to beams,
while up walls thick with rustling field mouse
and pursuing black snake our boys clambered
to Tarzan with the rooftree-high hung rope
wall-to-wall in ever widening arcs
as through the winter tier by tier we tore
their castle down and flung it to the cows .

By spring the boys' towered ramparts lay
scattered on floor so thick with broken bales
they took to sleeping there, doors flung open
to fields gold-gilded by a moon full
and yellow as the grass they lay upon.

The Slaughter of Innocents

This year the wild cat had her litter
underneath the garden shed,
abandoning to ants the two
whose eyes would never open.

No one has use for such as they,
and so I swaddled and laid them
in a bucket filled with water
and sat myself upon its lid

the longest minutes I have sat
until I knew them drowned for sure,
then took the sodden blanket out
and buried all behind the shed.

Killing mice

1

Insomniac at 3 a.m., I catch
mice scratching as they climb inside the walls
and know tomorrow I will read their track

in nibbled soap, turds in the silver drawer,
bites bit in potato, apple, onion,
holes in the rice and flour and sugar sacks,

bring out the traps and cheese, and the next
begin the morning burial patrol.
The lucky die but once, necks snapped, backs broke,

but those caught but by a leg or tail
dance till dawn with wooded-footed death.
Exhausted but alive, they die by brick.

2

Preferring long distance executions,
I condemn my uninvited guests
to lingering death by thirst and poison

somewhere out there beyond my pale and ken.
But some, insidious even unto death,
refuse to quit the premises and die within.

Who knew the rotting carcass of a mouse
could turn a home into a charnel house,
or that its memory could so foul mine?

Paint and perfume though I will, and family
and friend pretend to notice nothing,
I know the walls behind which still lie bones.

3

The cat kills nightly, disemboweling
her prey and dropping it as gift or insult
on floor and stair for master to dispose.

Invisibly the screech owl terrifies
both mouse and man, and from the fields arrives
the black snake seeking supper in my house.

Grabbed, her muscular six feet so caress,
embrace, then kiss the body carrying hers
back to the garden that it remembers

long the feel of her cold length around it,
her tongue that would taste his, her yellow eyes
regarding his, her scent that lingered days.

Haying

We hayed in early June this year,
the waist-high, heavy-headed grass
tickling the green belly of the tractor
as the sicklebar clacked and clattered

to the grass it cut and lay
to dry in yellowing windrows,
and flushed the hidden deer away,
and chased the larks into the sky.

We returned and with the side rake
fluffed and pillowed up the hay
until the spinning pinwheels choked
and threw towards the sun the body

of a fawn the bar caught and killed
as it shrank its spotted flanks
into its mother's still warm bed
and watched the sickle scatter grass

and flower as it carved its way
towards its unintended prey.

Fireflies

Remember when you learned at last
the knack of catching fireflies
and through the ankle-tickling grass
chased their elusive fairy lights?

How you ran and ran that night
ignoring shadows in the yard
and slept, a jam jar filled with light
grasped tight in fingers green with gore?

How you rose the morrow morn
to a jam jar dark and dead
and overheard your life's lid turn
and caught your breath on air gone stale?

Others

We started at the river, in shade so thick
the ground lay open like a park,
then panted up, up, up the mountain's flank,
its sandstone bones but barely covered
by a skin of stunted pine and huckleberry
to view the Valley splayed below us—
so like my hand's climb through the fine fur of your pelvis,
the color of fallen pine needles,
its ridgeline curving up, up and around,
the Blue Ridge of your breasts visible
across the plain of your chest.
I thought we had outpaced all others,
until I spied a candy wrapper there
and here your husband's photo on the shelf.

Sugar Creek

The county map quite clearly indicates
Sugar Creek flows here, though it appears
its waters slipped this narrow bed
dry and cracked as last year's snake skin
to slither down between the cobbles
and bathe in undiscovered caves
where stalactites heavy with desire
yearn earthward eyed by things
grown blind forgetful of the light,
the creek's pulse faint as a heartbeat
overheard through blouse or shirt,
its course as secret as the blood's
beneath the skin.

Like or As

When you rise to pee at night
I think your ass most like
the rising moon rising, trailing clouds of bedclothes,
the sun curtained by a negligee of fog,
or a pear, a perfect pear upon a perfect branch,
ripe, soft, and yielding to my touch,
or canned, perhaps, naked upon my plate,
its bare flesh swimming in heavy syrup,
your cheek's sweet swell most like a peeled avocado,
or a garlic bulb stripped of its paper petticoat
and sensible underwear of skin, bare cloves curving
damp and delicious in the dark,
a hot air balloon aglow at twilight,
a single Chinese lantern in the night,
a citronella candle guttering in its globe,
a naked lamp bulb hanging from the ceiling of my mind.
Then you return and nestle into me
like a teaspoon in the silver drawer,
rump cool and smooth as river rock,
as ripe watermelon flush with summer's sweetmeat,
as a plump pumpkin whose ridgeline seduces
me to another body part and poem.

Successor

Should I, at three a.m.,
pee loudly in the bowl,
force you to listen while
I doglike mark it?
or aim for the side,
spare you another male
staking his territory?
In either case, we'll both flush,
and you'll recall
another's emptying bladder,
as I imagine
another gazing sadly out this window
at the empty sky and fields.

Feeding the fire

Feeding the fire,
she sits upon a bench,
legs apart,
lifting the split logs
one by one
into the fire box.
The heat embraces her,
hot hands on her knees,
fingers insinuating
between her bathrobe's folds,
climbing her thighs
cool and smooth as beech bark
towards her pubic forest—
dark, naked trees
against the full moon of her skin.

Landscapes

When you lie flat
upon your back in bed,
your breasts seem a girl's
on the cusp of puberty,
to the fast traveling eye
like minor hills
rising from the Kansas of your chest.
But I have walked by hand those hills,
muscles aching like a boy
who undoes for the first time a bra
and discovers how perfectly
a girl's breast fills
his hollow hand's desire.

Conjugating Verbs

Painting, you chainsaw trees, bulldoze
hills, inventing cows and hay bales in craft
so devious your clients think you paint
what they see outside their picture windows,

like the deceptions we all play upon
ourselves, remembering as in a film
ourselves outside ourselves, driving a car
or eating lunch, or this: kissing, eyes closed,

your breast and seeing it more perfect than
an air-brushed foldout's, more perfect than that
your first lover first saw forty years ago,
yours perfect, past perfect, future perfect.

Morning Breath

Sleeping skin, freed from the prison
of the guarded self, relaxes,
childhood's unself-conscious face
bleeding through like a familiar stain.
And from barely parted lips
adulthood's odor oozes,
slight as a half remembered memory,
like the whiff a passing car admits
of a bloat deer
dead upon the roadside.

To Wit

When I am dead,
by actuarial count
in fifteen years,
you will not know,
not even guess,
unless by codicil,
that I am gone
to an eternal bedding down
no colder than this
I now alone endure.
And, therefore, item:
To my once dear wife,
I leave my memory.
May she treat it more kindly
than I did her.
Together we could not stand
each other,
apart I could not stand
myself,
and now I lie alone.

Reliquary

A fond old man, I climb these steepening stairs
to an attic you have never visited,
to a box you've never seen,
to relics you have long forgot—
a lone earring, a necklace, clasp broken,
this brush stranded with your hair,
this mothbit sweater to which still clings
like hope the memory of your scent,
this, your last supper's plate,
and this, the cup you drank,
and this, the napkin your lips kissed,
parsing your parting words
for what I know cannot,
but must, be there—
the promise of your soon return.

Silly Goose

Lose me though I do in the mindless day-
 to-day of work, mornings when I wake
 and overhear geese veeing south to lakes
without ice, I float fifty years away
 to waiting winter mornings for the bus
while above the lowering clouds, the great birds
called come away, come away. Long dead,
those great, great grand progenitors accuse
me still of having chosen this kitchen
 window out of which I dream what might have been.
Rising large and dark against my low horizons,
they wing it towards pastures new and dawn,
abandoning me here, in this, my life,
with the dung they drop when taking off.

Grey Days

Winter when clouds hang lower than my soul,
the trucks on 81 hum come away,
and I dream me south to Florida's
great, tropic-reaching length, a thousand miles
of palms down to the Keys, where it all ends
in ever summer land. Then I envy
slowpoking snowbirds cramped within RVs,
and price the sites at KOA campgrounds.
The truckstop never stops, and so I'm here
at 3 a.m., the purring semis lit
like carnival, their cowboy-booted
drivers on their ways to someplace, somewhere
else momentarily seducing me
to think escape a possibility.

Monarchs

Monarchs ride fall's cold fronts south in waves,
warming us in thin orange blankets stitched
by a million nearly mindless threads
weaving arabesques bright as autumn leaves.
I too would leave, run with the wind, and wave
goodbye to all of this, fly a carpet
over the Appalachians' parapets,
high above the Mississippi's swerves,
head south to the Gulf and west to Texas,
crossing the Rio in a grander, drier river,
through Chihuahua, Durango, Zacatecas,
into Michoacan's fabled forest firs
and winter where the trees are hung with wealth
undreamt by Bogarts mucking gold beneath.

Middle-Aged Romance

Whose faces face us when, eyes closed, we kiss?
Do you too remember lovers unseen
for years, in memory alive and young,
but, in truth, old now, and dead perhaps?
Not as many as we might have wished,
but enough to make us, if not perfect,
then practiced. Enough as well to make us cheats,
though what we cheat's uncertain as first kisses,
and those we doubted even as we embraced,
wondering how who we kissed knew how to kiss,
we but the latest love, desire our desire,
to be desired by whom we desired,
to want who wanted us, to want no more
than this, to want no more, to want to want no more.

Bluebeard

I now love girls younger than my daughter,
long-haired revenants from long ago
kept captive in the family photo album
yellowed as old teeth and faded paper.

They're all here, in the mind's multiplex,
undying loves in roles impossible,
all these teasing trailers to my coming
attractions, no act complete, no climax,

love scenes so cinematized as to suppose
the willing suspension of disbelief,
like the twenty seconds of imagined love
you feed with quarters at the carnie shows.

Film them though I would, my starlets refuse
my camera eye, turning their gaze on me,
love after testifying love crying
from the witness box, j'accuse, j'accuse, j'accuse.

Guilty? Of course I'm guilty. Aren't we all?
How else explain these carcasses of lost loves
we gut sleepless nights and hang to blue,
flyblown and filthy, on our attic walls?

Lullaby

Sleeping on my faithless arm
dream of surer loves than ours,
morning may you wake once more
in a world that holds no harm.

Last night's desperate passion spent
purchase you no lasting sorrow,
infidelity tomorrow
lodge against my heart's account.

When through future nights you lie
in another love's embrace,
may you not dream of my face
guarding yours with open eye.

Three A.M.

Three A.M. and drunk
are two bad reasons
to learn again,
and over the phone,
she still thinks she was right
to break it off.
Far better she sleep and you talk
with memory instead.
Now there's someone
we've all taken calls from late at night.
All she wants is you, sleepless,
and here she is,
in bed and ready
to rehash every wrong and wasted love.
Long or short,
it doesn't matter,
they're all here,
every time,
every one
you ever hurt, loved, lost, betrayed, abandoned,
disappointed, let down, disgusted, failed
—fill in your own damn verb,
this is my phone call, after all—
enough to fill the bed and room,
broken hearts squat on the television,
two or three you wronged Tarzaning on the curtains,
a legion of loves lost wailing in the closet,
and the bed chockablock with outrage.
Time? That's all you've got left now,

time and the memories.
And if you thought marriage an eternity,
try three A.M.

Kissing

Should we two ever kiss again,
let it be, eyes opened.
Though first love's fumbled kiss be lost
and perfect kisses mouth our many cheats,
we shall then conjure no one but ourselves,
should we two ever kiss again.